Decorator THROWS

The Best of Mary Maxim®

I0893778

LEISURE ARTS, INC. • Maumelle, Arkansas

Aran Textures and Cables Afghan and Pillow

INTERMEDIATE

SHOPPING LIST

Yarn (Worsted Weight) MEDIUM 4

Mary Maxim Starlette
[3.5 ounces, 180 yards
(100 grams, 165 meters) per ball]:

☐ 15 balls

Knitting Needles

36" (90 cm) Circular Needle

☐ Size 9 (5.50 mm)
or size needed for gauge

Additional Supply

18" (45.5 cm) Pillow form

SIZE INFORMATION

Finished:

Afghan 48" x 60" [122 x 152.5 cm]
Pillow 18" [45.5 cm] Square

GAUGE INFORMATION

Gauge: 12 sts and 18 rows to 3" [7.5 cm] measured over Box Stitch; Cable and Eyelet Panel = 2¼" [5.5 cm] wide, Open Work Panel = 6¼" [16 cm] wide, and Tri Cable Panel = 3" [7.5 cm] wide, all using **suggested** needle or any size needle which will give the correct stitch gauge or tension.

TO SAVE TIME, TAKE TIME TO CHECK GAUGE

STITCH GUIDE

M1 - Make one stitch: Using left-hand needle, lift the yarn laying between the stitch just worked and the next stitch, then knit into back of this loop.

PM - Place marker.

SM - Slip marker.

ssk - slip, slip, knit: Slip next 2 sts knitwise, one at a time, to right needle, then insert left needle through both sts from back to front and knit sts together as usual.

C4B - Cable 4 Back: Slip next 2 sts onto cable needle and hold to back of work, k2 from left-hand needle, then k2 from cable needle.

PATTERN STITCHES

Box Stitch Pattern:

Row 1: *P3, k3; rep from * to last 3 sts, p3.

Row 2: *K3, p3; rep from * to last 3 sts, k3.

Rows 3 and 4: Repeat Rows 1 & 2 once more.

Row 5: As Row 2.

Row 6: As Row 1.

Rows 7 and 8: Repeat Rows 5 & 6 once more.

Repeat these 8 rows for Box Stitch Pattern.

Cable and Eyelet Pattern: (Worked over 14 sts)

Row 1: (right side) P1, k4, p1, k2tog, yo, p1, k4, p1.

Rows 2, 4 and 6: K1, p4, k1, p2, k1, p4, k1.

Row 3: P1, C4B, p1, yo, ssk, p1, C4B, p1.

Row 5: As Row 1.

Row 7: P1, k4, p1, yo, ssk, p1, k4, p1.

Row 8: As Row 2.

Repeat these 8 rows for Cable and Eyelet Pattern.

Open Work Pattern:

Row 1: (right side) P1, k1, *yo, k3, then with left-hand needle, lift the first of these three sts just worked over the last 2; rep from * to one st before next marker, p1.

Row 2: K1, purl to one st before next marker, k1.

Row 3: P1, *k3, then with left-hand needle, lift the first of these three sts just worked over the last 2, yo; rep from * to last 2 sts before next marker, k1, p1.

Row 4: As Row 2.

Repeat these 4 rows for Open Work Pattern.

Tri Cable Pattern: (Worked over 20 sts)

Rows 1, 5, 9, 13, 17 and 21: (right side) P2, *k4, p2; rep from * to next marker.

Row 2 and all even rows: K2, *p4, k2; rep from * to next marker.

Rows 3, 7 and 11: P2, k4, p2, C4B, p2, k4, p2.

Rows 15, 19 and 23: P2, C4B, p2, k4, p2, C4B, p2.

Row 24: K2, *p4, k2; rep from * to next marker.

Repeat these 24 rows for Tri Cable Pattern.

Afghan

Lower Border: Cast on 207 sts and working back and forth on circular needle, work 12 rows of Box Stitch for Lower Border.

The first and last 9 sts will continue in Box Stitch throughout the entire Afghan.

In the next row, markers will be placed and increases made, to set up the various patterns.

Row 13: (inc Row, right side) Work first 9 sts in Box Stitch as established, PM, [k1, M1] twice, k2, k into front and back of next st, k2, [M1, k1] twice; PM, work in Box Stitch over next 9 sts, PM, p1, k1, [yo, k3, then with left-hand needle lift the first of these three sts just worked over the last 2] 8 times, p1, PM, work Box Stitch over next 9 sts, PM, p1, [k into front and back of next st, k2] 4 times, k into front and back of next st, p1, PM, work Box Stitch over next 9 sts, PM, p1, k1, [yo, k3, then with left-hand needle lift the first of these three sts just worked over the last 2] 10 times, p1, PM, work Box Stitch Pattern over next 9 sts, PM, p1, [k into front and back of next st, k2] 4 times, k into front and back of next st, p1, PM, work Box Stitch over next 9 sts, PM, p1, k1, [yo, k3, then with left-hand needle lift the first of these three sts just worked over the last 2] 8 times, p1, PM, work Box Stitch over next 9 sts, PM, [k1, M1] twice, k2, k into front and back of next st, k2, [M1, k1] twice, PM, work Box Stitch over next 9 sts - 227 sts.

Row 14: Work Box Stitch to first marker, SM, work Row 2 of Cable and Eyelet to next marker, SM, work Box Stitch to next marker, SM, work Row 2 of Open Work to next marker, SM, work Box Stitch to next marker, SM, work Row 2 of Tri Cable Pattern to next marker, SM, work Box Stitch to next marker, SM, work Row 2 of Open Work to next marker, SM, work Box Stitch to next marker, SM, work Row 2 of Tri Cable Pattern to next marker, SM, work Box Stitch to next marker, SM, work Row 2 of Open Work to next marker, SM, work Box Stitch to next marker, SM, work Row 2 of Cable and Eyelet to next marker, SM, work Box Stitch to end.

Row 15: Work patterns as established across the needle, keeping Box Stitch Pattern correct and working Row 3 of each of the other patterns, slipping markers as you go.

Row 16: Work patterns as established across the needle, keeping Box Stitch Pattern correct and working Row 4 of each of the other patterns, slipping markers as you go.

Now continue working patterns as established, working through all rows of each pattern, until 24 rows of the Tri Cable Pattern have been completed 13 times; then continue working all patterns, until Rows 1-11 of the Tri Cable Pattern have been completed once more.

Next Row: (dec row, wrong side) Work Box Stitch over first 9 sts, k1, [p2tog] twice, k1, p2tog, k1, [p2tog] twice, k1, Box Stitch over next 9 sts, k1, p 25, k1, Box Stitch over next 9 sts, k2, [p2tog] twice, k2, p1, p2tog, p1, k2, [p2tog] twice, k2, Box Stitch over next 9 sts, k1, p 31, k1, Box Stitch over next 9 sts, k2, [p2tog] twice, k2, p1, p2tog, p1, k2, [p2tog] twice, k2, Box Stitch over next 9 sts, k1, p 25, k1, Box Stitch over next 9 sts, k1, [p2tog] twice, k1, p2tog, k1, [p2tog] twice, k1, Box Stitch to end - 207 sts.

Upper Border: Now Box Stitch over all sts, until 12 rows have been completed. Cast off knitwise.

Fringe: If desired, fringe is attached to each end of afghan, with one tassel in the middle of each 3-stitch group in the Box Stitch Pattern.

There are 69 tassels at each end of the afghan.

Cut 276 pieces, each 10" [25.5 cm] in length.

Take 4 strands for each tassel.

Fold strands in half to make a loop, making sure ends are even. Insert crochet hook through the edge of the afghan, in the middle stitch of a group of 3; then insert hook into loop formed by folded strands. Use hook to pull this loop through edge of afghan far enough that fingers can then be used to pull cut ends of strands through the yarn loop to knot the tassel. Pull all the strands carefully through, tightening evenly. Repeat this process across the lower and upper ends of the afghan.

Trim ends to neaten.

Fringe

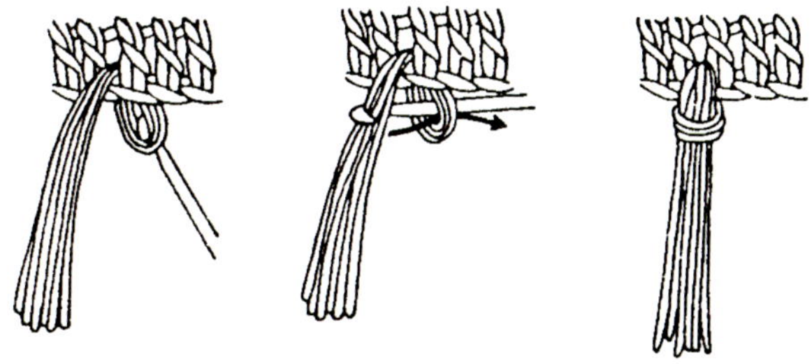

Pillow

To Make: Cast on 86 sts.

Row 1: (right side) P1, *k4, p1, k2tog, yo, p1; rep from * to last 5 sts, k4, p1.

Rows 2, 4 and 6: K1, *p4, k1, p2, k1; rep from * to last 5 sts, p4, k1.

Row 3: P1, *C4B, p1, yo, ssk, p1; rep from * to last 5 sts, C4B, p1.

Row 5: As Row 1.

Row 7: P1, *k4, p1, yo, ssk, p1; rep from * to last 5 sts, k4, p1.

Row 8: As Row 2.

Repeat these 8 rows, 22 times more. Then rep Rows 1 through 7 once more.

Next Row: (dec row, wrong side) K1, p1, p2tog, p1, *k1, p2tog, k1, p1, p2tog, p1; rep from * to last st, k1 - 65 sts.

Next Row: K1, work Box Stitch to last st, k1.

Continue working the next rows of Box Stitch Pattern, completing 12 rows and knitting the first and last sts of each row.

Cast off knitwise.

To Complete: Using a yarn needle, slip st dec row to cast on edge, forming a tube.

Slip pillow form inside.

Center the Box Stitch Pattern across middle of pillow, and sew side seams.

Sew in all ends.

Box Stitch section will form a flap. If desired, fringe is now added to the edge of this section.

Fringe: Cut 84 pieces, each 7" [18 cm] in length. Using 4 strands for each tassel, make fringe as given for the Afghan, attaching it to the small flap across the front of the pillow.

Design by Mary K. Hobbs.

Log Cabin Throw

INTERMEDIATE

SHOPPING LIST

Yarn (Worsted Weight) MEDIUM 4

Mary Maxim Starlette

[3.5 ounces, 180 yards

(100 grams, 165 meters) per ball]:

- ☐ Color 1 Dk Coral 2 balls
- ☐ Color 2 Green 2 balls
- ☐ Color 3 Blue 3 balls
- ☐ Color 4 Tan 2 balls
- ☐ Color 5 Red 2 balls
- ☐ Color 6 Brown 2 balls

Knitting Needles

36" (90 cm) Circular Needle

- ☐ Size 9 (5.50 mm)

SIZE INFORMATION

Finished: 46" x 50" [117 x 127 cm]

GAUGE INFORMATION

16 sts and 31 rows to 4" [10 cm] measured over Garter stitch using **suggested** needles or any size needles which will give the correct gauge.

TO SAVE TIME, TAKE TIME TO CHECK GAUGE

INSTRUCTIONS

Note: Use pair of straight needles until you find the number of sts too much to handle, then switch to circular needle. Continue to work back and forth on circular needle, Do Not join.

Center Block: Using Color 3 and straight needles, cast on 40 sts. Work in Garter st - every row knit, marking first row as a right side row, until block measures 14" [35.5 cm] from beg, working an even number of rows. Do not cast off.

Strip 2: Using Color 1, k 12 rows.

**Now continue in the following color sequence and knit 12 rows of each color: Color 2; Color 3; Color 4; Color 5, then Color 6.

Cast off on last row of Color 6.**

Strip 3: Using Color 1, with right side facing (refer to Placement Diagram on page 8), pick up and k 36 sts down left side of Strip 2, 54 sts down left side of Center Block (pick up one st for each ridge) - 90 sts.

Knit 11 rows.

Now work as given for Strip 2 from ** to **.

Strip 4: Using Color 1, with right side facing (refer to Placement Diagram), pick up and k 36 sts along side of Strip 3, and 40 sts across bottom of Center Block (pick up one st for each ridge) - 76 sts.

Knit 11 rows.

Now work as given for Strip 2 from ** to **.

Strip 5: Using Color 1, with right side facing (refer to Placement Diagram), pick up and k 36 sts along side of Strip 4, 54 sts along side of Center Block, and 36 sts along side of Strip 2 (pick up one st for each ridge) - 126 sts.

Knit 11 rows.

Now work as given for Strip 2 from ** to **.

Strip 6: Using Color 1, with right side facing (refer to Placement Diagram), pick up and k 36 sts along side of Strip 5, 40 sts across top of Strip 2, and 36 sts along side of Strip 3 (pick up one st for each ridge) - 112 sts.

Knit 11 rows.

Now work as given for Strip 2 from ** to **.

Strip 7: Using Color 1, with right side facing (refer to Placement Diagram), pick up and k 36 sts along side of Strip 6, 90 sts across top of Strip 3, and 36 sts along side of Strip 4 (pick up one st for each ridge) - 162 sts.

Knit 11 rows.

Now work as given for Strip 2 from ** to **.

Strip 8: Using Color 1, with right side facing (refer to Placement Diagram), pick up and k 36 sts along side of Strip 7, 76 sts across top of Strip 4, and 36 sts along side of Strip 5 (pick up one st for each ridge) - 148 sts.

Knit 11 rows.

Now work as given for Strip 2 from ** to **.

Strip 9: Using Color 1, with right side facing (refer to Placement Diagram), pick up and k 36 sts along side of Strip 8, 126 sts across top of Strip 5, and 36 sts along side of Strip 6 (pick up one st for each ridge) - 198 sts.

Knit 11 rows.

Now work as given for Strip 2 from ** to **.

Weave in all ends.

Placement Diagram

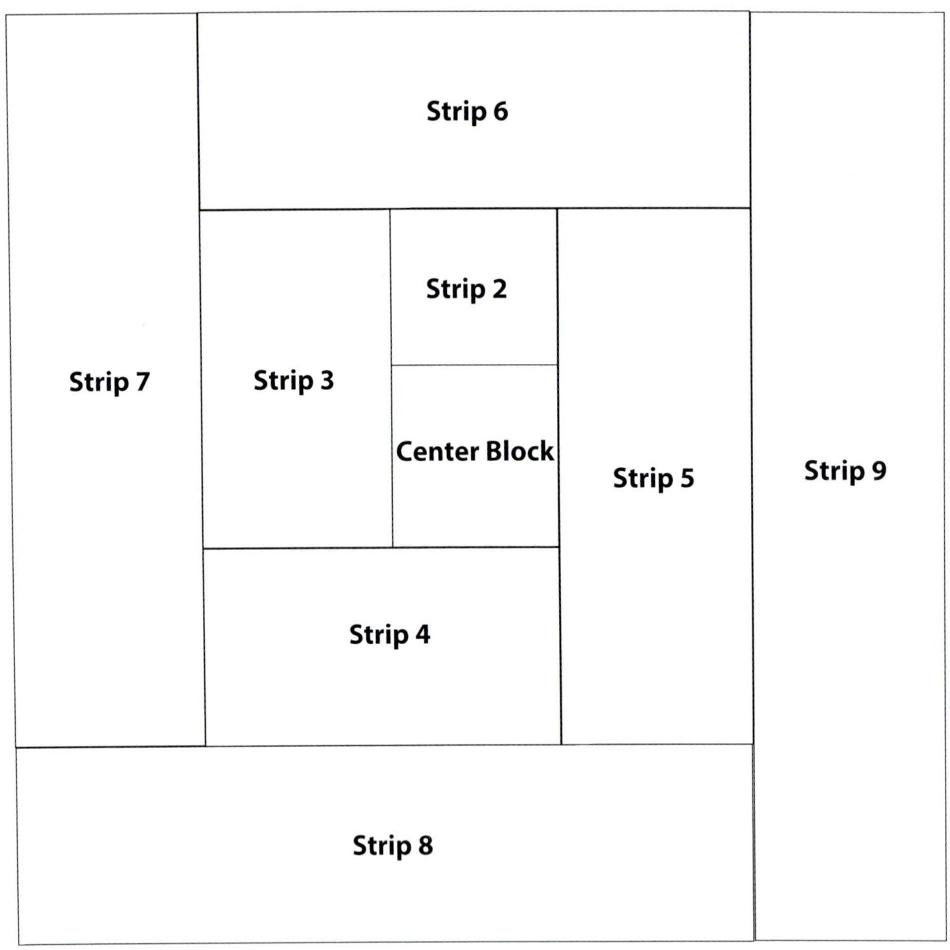

Zig Zag Throw

EASY

SHOPPING LIST

Yarn (Worsted Weight) MEDIUM 4

Mary Maxim Best Value

[6 ounces, 315 yards

(170 grams, 288 meters) per skein]:

- ☐ Color 1 Merlot 3 skeins
- ☐ Color 2 Misty Plum 3 skeins
- ☐ Color 3 Cottonwood 2 skeins

Knitting Needles

- ☐ Size 7 (4.50 mm)

SIZE INFORMATION

Finished: 40" x 52" [101.5 x 132 cm]

GAUGE INFORMATION

20 sts and 28 rows to 4" [10 cm] measured over Garter stitch using **suggested** needles or any size needles which will give the correct stitch gauge or tension.

TO SAVE TIME, TAKE TIME TO CHECK GAUGE

STITCH GUIDE

SKP: Slip 1 knitwise, k1, pass slipped stitch over k1.

INSTRUCTIONS

Work 5 panels in total - 2 each in Colors 1 and 2, then one in Color 3.

To Make Panel: Cast on 35 sts, and knit 11 rows (for border). Now work pattern as follows:

Row 1 and every alternate row: K7, [p7, k7] twice.

Row 2: (right side) K 11, k2tog, yo, k 12, k2tog, yo, k8.

Row 4: K 10, k2tog, yo, k 12, k2tog, yo, k9.

Row 6: K9, k2tog, yo, k 12, k2tog, yo, k 10.

Row 8: K8, k2tog, yo, k 12, k2tog, yo, k 11.

Row 10: K7, [k2tog, yo, k 12] twice.

Row 12: K8, yo, SKP, k 12, yo, SKP, k 11.

Row 14: K9, yo, SKP, k 12, yo, SKP, k 10.

Row 16: K 10, yo, SKP, k 12, yo, SKP, k9.

Row 18: K 11, yo, SKP, k 12, yo, SKP, k8.

Row 20: [K 12, yo, SKP] twice, k7.

Repeat these 20 rows for pattern 17 times.

Panel should measure approximately 51½" [131 cm] in length.

Knit 11 rows. Cast off knitwise.

To Assemble:

Lay panels on a flat surface with right sides facing upwards, in the following color order, Color 1, Color 2, Color 3, Color 2, Color 1. Sew panels together lengthwise, being sure to keep all panels the same length.

Design by Jeannine LaRoche.

Cable Panels Throw

INTERMEDIATE

SHOPPING LIST

Yarn (Worsted Weight) MEDIUM 4

Mary Maxim Starlette

[3.5 ounces, 180 yards

(100 grams, 165 meters) per ball]:

☐ Color 1	Russet	2 balls
☐ Color 2	Blue	2 balls
☐ Color 3	Green	2 balls
☐ Color 4	Plum	2 balls

Knitting Needles

☐ Size 8 (5.00 mm)

SIZE INFORMATION

Finished: 36" x 46" [91.5 x 117 cm]

GAUGE INFORMATION

One panel measures 9" [23 cm] wide and 24 rows measures 4 1/4" [11 cm], using the **suggested** needles or any size needles which will give the correct stitch gauge or tension.

TO SAVE TIME, TAKE TIME TO CHECK GAUGE

STITCH GUIDE

C8B - Cable 8 Back: Slip next 4 sts onto cable needle and hold to back of work, k4 from left-hand needle, then k4 from cable needle.

INSTRUCTIONS

Panel: (make 4, one in each color)

Using Color 1, cast on 38 sts and knit 7 rows.

Next Row: K6, [knit into front and back of next st] 4 times, k 18, [knit into front and back of next st] 4 times, k6 - 46 sts.

Now work in pattern as follows:

Row 1: (right side) K4, p2, k8, p2, k2tog, k5, yo, k2tog, yo, k1, yo, k2, sl 1, k1, psso, p2, k8, p2, k4.

Row 2: K6, p8, k2, p 14, k2, p8, k6.

Row 3: K4, p2, k8, p2, k2tog, k4, yo, k2tog, yo, k3, yo, k1, sl 1, k1, psso, p2, k8, p2, k4.

Row 4: Work as Row 2.

Row 5: K4, p2, C8B, p2, k2tog, k3, yo, k2tog, yo, k5, yo, sl 1, k1, psso, p2, C8B, p2, k4.

Row 6: Work as Row 2.

Row 7: K4, p2, k8, p2, k2tog, k2, yo, k1, yo, sl 1, k1, psso, yo, k5, sl 1, k1, psso, p2, k8, p2, k4.

Row 8: Work as Row 2.

Row 9: K4, p2, k8, p2, k2tog, k1, yo, k3, yo, sl 1, k1, psso, yo, k4, sl 1, k1, psso, p2, k8, p2, k4.

Row 10: Work as Row 2.

Row 11: K4, p2, k8, p2, k2tog, yo, k5, yo, sl 1, k1, psso, yo, k3, sl 1, k1, psso, p2, k8, p2, k4.

Row 12: Work as Row 2.

Repeat these 12 rows of pattern 20 times more, then rep Rows 1-7 once more.

Next Row: K6, [k2tog] 4 times, k 18, [k2tog] 4 times, k6 - 38 sts.

Knit 7 rows. Cast off knitwise.

Repeat using rem 3 colors.

To Assemble: Using color picture as a guide, sew panels together neatly.

Lighthouses Afghan

INTERMEDIATE

SHOPPING LIST

Yarn (Worsted Weight) MEDIUM 4

Red Heart® Super Saver®

[7 ounces, 364 yards

(198 grams, 333 meters) per skein]:

☐ Main Color	White	3 skeins
☐ Color 1	Lt Blue	2 skeins
☐ Color 2	Dk Blue	1 skein
☐ Color 3	Dk Brown	1 skein
☐ Color 4	Lt Green	120 yds (109m)
☐ Color 5	Dk Green	120 yds (109m)
☐ Color 6	Sand	120 yds (109m)
☐ Color 7	Lt Brown	160 yds (146m)
☐ Color 8	Yellow	120 yds (109m)
☐ Color 9	Red	120 yds (109m)
☐ Color 10	Lt Grey	120 yds (109m)
☐ Color 11	Med Grey	120 yds (109m)
☐ Color 12	Black	40 yds (36m)

Knitting Needles

☐ Size 7 (4.50 mm)

SIZE INFORMATION

Finished: approx. 58½" x 47" [148.5 x 119 cm]

GAUGE INFORMATION

18 sts and 24 rows to 4" [10 cm] measured over Stocking stitch using **suggested** needles or any size needles which will give the correct stitch gauge.

TO SAVE TIME, TAKE TIME TO CHECK GAUGE

STITCH GUIDE

How to Work Design:

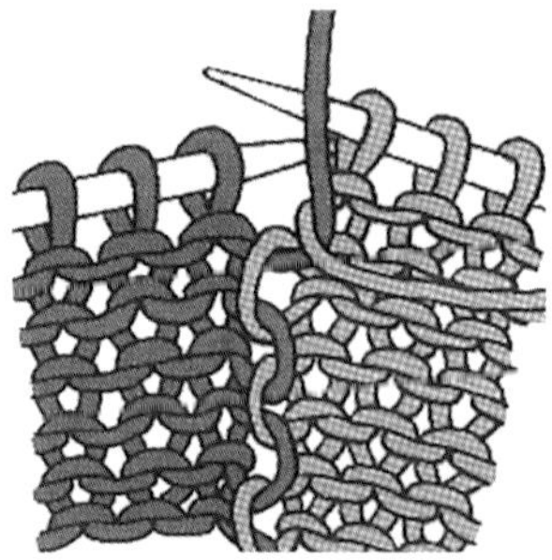

Colored Pattern Knitting: This method is used for large areas of each color and background, using small balls of color for each area. Work required number of sts, drop color in use to be picked up on next row, bring new color under and over last color, thus avoiding a hole in the knitting.

How to Sew Seams:

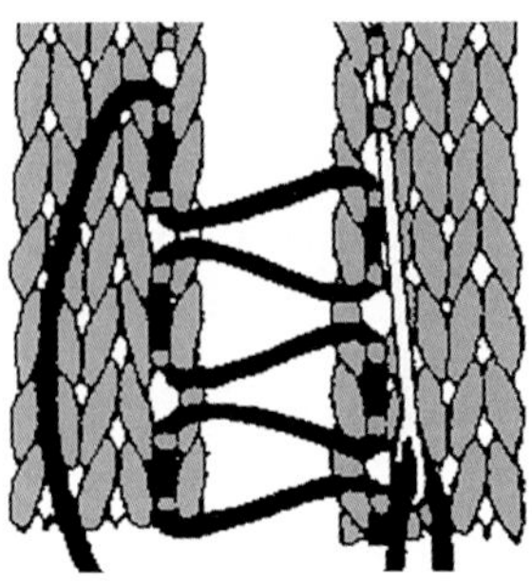

When sewing the pieces together, make sure to use the very first stitch of each piece to form the seams. This will allow the afghan to lay flat and there will not be ridges of seams on the back side of the afghan. Take time when sewing this afghan together and make all seams nice, neat and invisible as possible.

INSTRUCTIONS

Note: It is important that all squares finish to the same size, so adjust your needle size as needed. This also applies to the borders.

Graph 1: Using Color 3, cast on 41 sts loosely. Knit 4 rows. Now beg with a k row, proceed to follow Graph 1 on page 14 in St st - one row k, one row p. Work design in "Colored Pattern Knitting" method, using separate balls of color for each section of the design. Remember always to cross yarns when changing colors to avoid leaving a hole in the knitting. When 50 rows of graph have been completed, change to Color 3 and knit 3 rows. Cast off loosely knitwise.

Side Borders: Using Color 3 and with right side facing, beg at bottom corner, pick up and k3 sts along border, pick up and k 38 sts evenly along side of square, pick up and k3 sts along border - 44 sts. Knit 3 rows. Cast off loosely knitwise. Repeat on other side.

Graphs 2-10: Work as given for Graph 1, but following the correct graph on pages 14-16.

Plain Square:
Make 10 plain squares, one in each of the following colors: Color 1, Color 2, Color 4, Color 5, Color 6, Color 7, Color 8, Color 9, Color 10 and Color 11.

To Make: Using one of the colors above, cast on 45 sts. Now beg with a k row, work in St st, until 57 rows have been completed. Cast off loosely purlwise. Repeat for the other 9 squares.

To Assemble: Using Placement Diagram on page 17, sew squares tog, having 5 squares wide and 4 squares high. When sewing squares together, take care to keep each piece square and match corners as closely as you can.

Left Side Border: **Using MC, cast on 4 sts and knit 40 rows.

Next Row: K4, turn; cast on 20 sts - 24 sts.

Next Row: (right side, needle does not turn) Knit.

Next Row: K4 (outside edge), p 20.

Repeat the last 2 rows three times more. Now beg with a right side row, proceed to follow Border Graph A on page 17 in St st, working design as before and keeping the 4 outside edge sts in Garter st, every row k until 18 rows have been completed.

Repeat these 18 rows, but working each anchor in the following color order: Color 3, Color 10, Color 9, Color 11, Color 12, Color 4, Color 8, Color 5, Color 6, Color 2, Color 7.

When 18 rows of the last rep have been completed, cast off 20 sts loosely, k4.

On rem 4 sts, k 40 rows. Cast off knitwise.**

Sew this border to the left side of the afghan, having the anchors fit between each corner.

The 40 rows of Garter st are to be used later.

See color key on page 17.

GRAPH 1

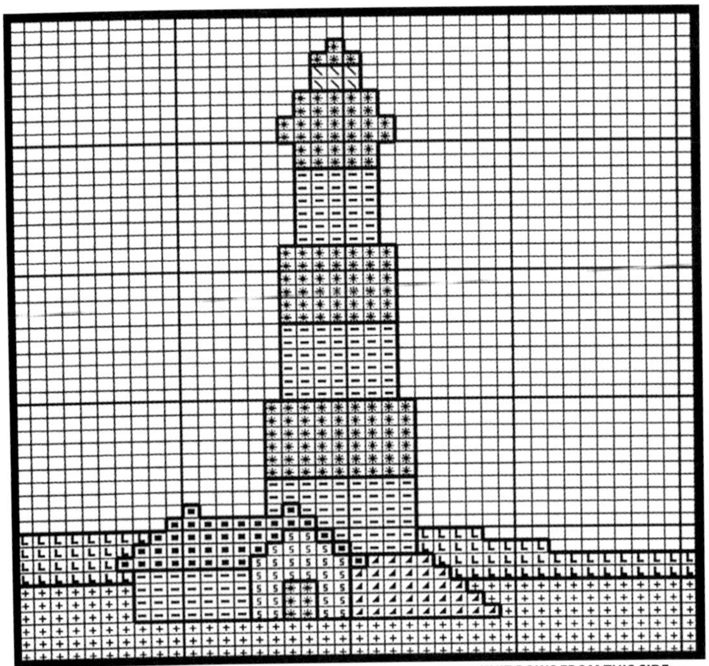

READ PURL ROWS FROM THIS SIDE READ KNIT ROWS FROM THIS SIDE

GRAPH 2

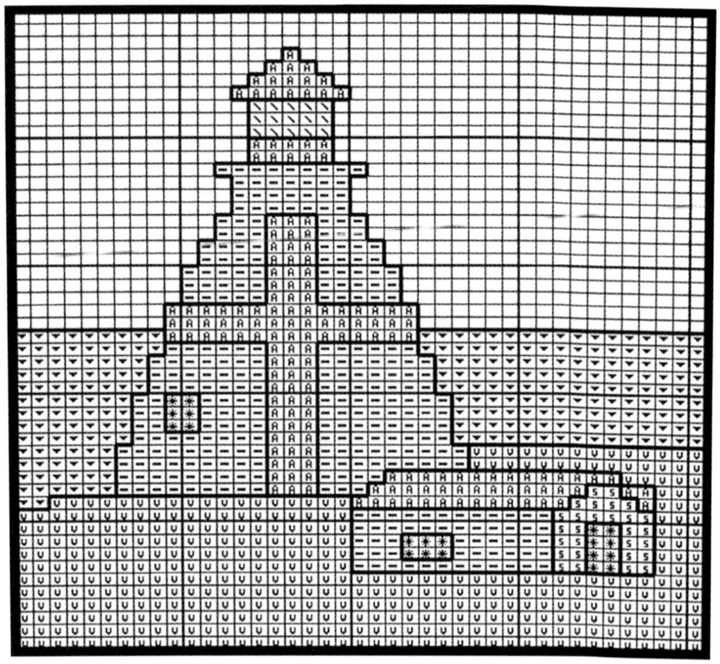

READ PURL ROWS FROM THIS SIDE READ KNIT ROWS FROM THIS SIDE

Top Border: **Using MC, cast on 24 sts loosely.

Beg with a right side row, proceed to follow Graph B on page 17, keeping last 4 sts in Garter st (outside edge) and working design as before.

When 32 rows of graph have been completed, rep Rows 15-32 of Graph B, but working each anchor in the following color order:

Color 10, Color 9, Color 11, Color 12, Color 4, Color 8, Color 5, Color 6, Color 2, Color 7, Color 1, Color 3, Color 10, Color 9, Color 11, Color 12.

When Row 32 of last rep has been completed, work last 4 rows of Graph B. Cast off.**

Sew this border to the top of the afghan, having Garter st as outside edge of border. Sew end of Top Border to 40 rows of Garter st from Left Side Border.

Right Side Border: Work as given for Left Side Border from ** to **, but working Graph C on page 17, then working rem anchors in the following color order: Color 8, Color 5, Color 6, Color 2, Color 7, Color 1, Color 3, Color 10, Color 9, Color 11, Color 12.

Sew this border to the right side of the afghan, having the anchors fit between each corner.

Sew end of Top Border to beg 40 rows of Garter st.

Bottom Border: Work from ** to ** as given for Top Border, but work anchors in the following color order from beg: Color 4, Color 8, Color 5, Color 6, Color 2, Color 7, Color 1, Color 3, Color 10, Color 9, Color 11, Color 12, Color 4, Color 8, Color 5, Color 6, Color 2, then Color 7.

Sew this border to bottom edge of afghan, having Garter st as outside edge of border. Sew both ends of Bottom Border to 40 rows of Garter st from Left Side and Right Side Borders.

Design by Joanna Bestward.

See color key on page 17.

GRAPH 3

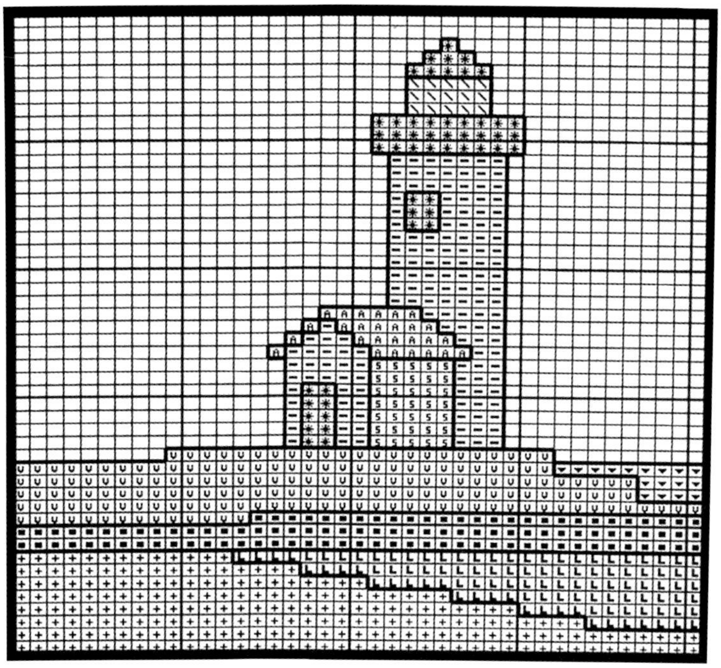

READ PURL ROWS FROM THIS SIDE | READ KNIT ROWS FROM THIS SIDE

GRAPH 4

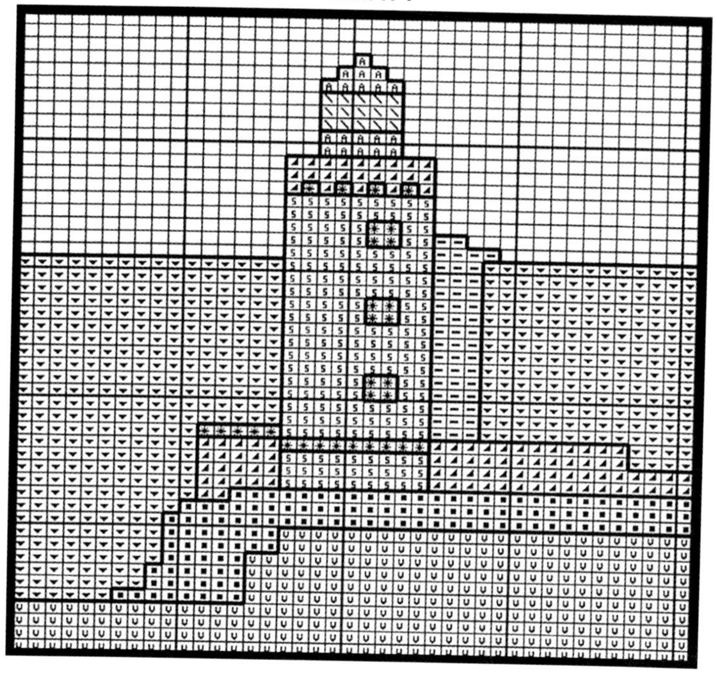

READ PURL ROWS FROM THIS SIDE | READ KNIT ROWS FROM THIS SIDE

GRAPH 5

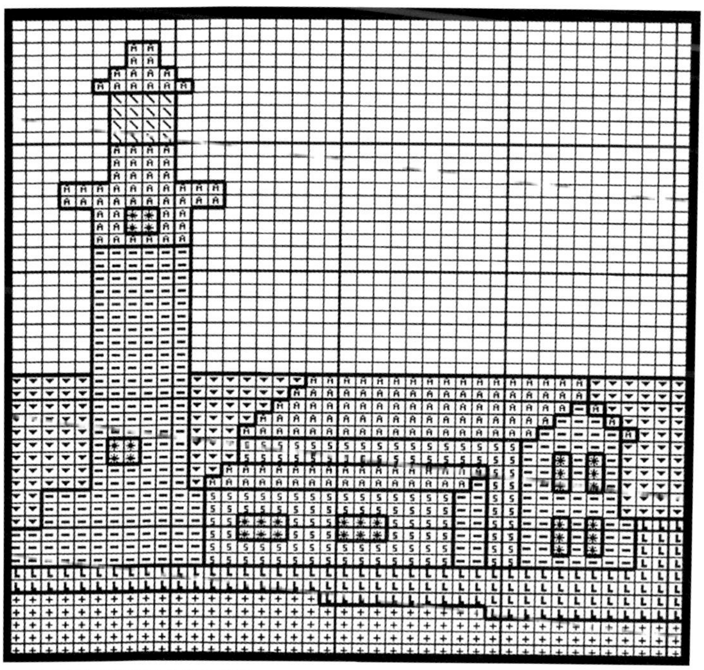

READ PURL ROWS FROM THIS SIDE | READ KNIT ROWS FROM THIS SIDE

GRAPH 6

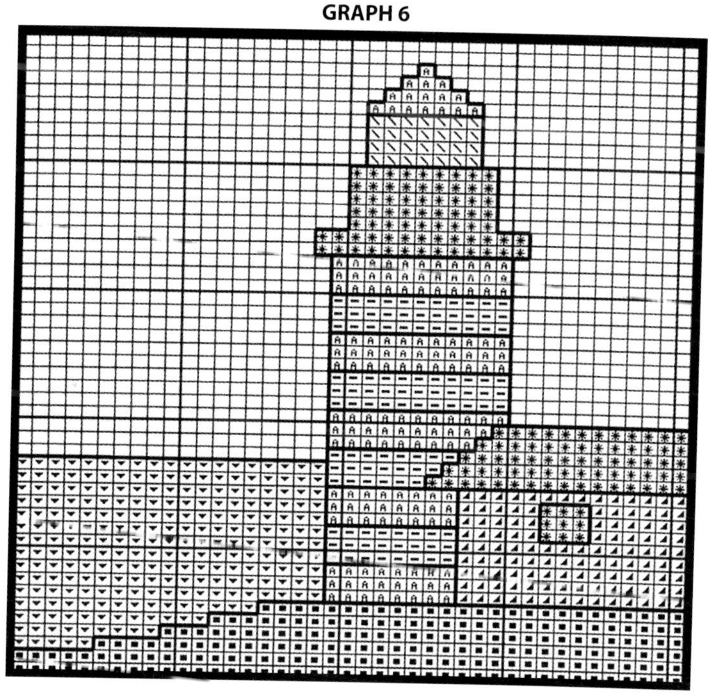

READ PURL ROWS FROM THIS SIDE | READ KNIT ROWS FROM THIS SIDE

GRAPH 7

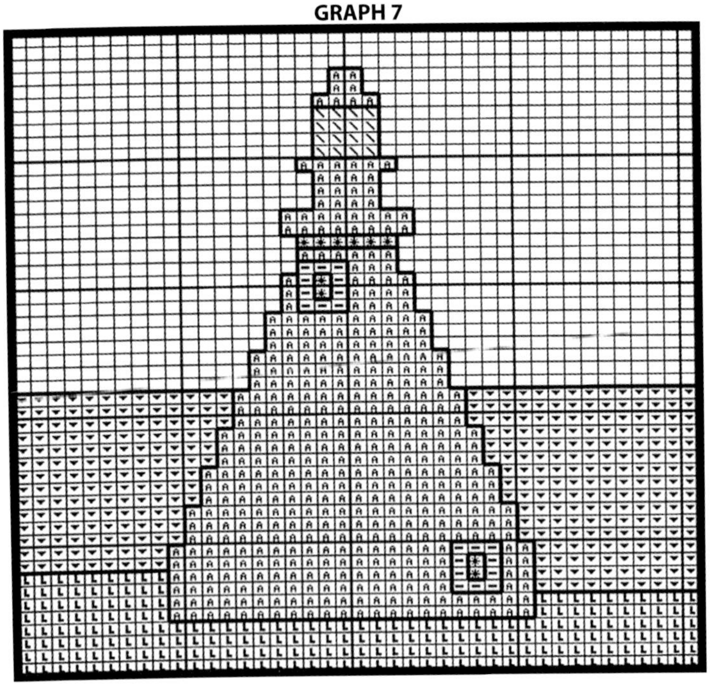

READ PURL ROWS FROM THIS SIDE

READ KNIT ROWS FROM THIS SIDE

GRAPH 8

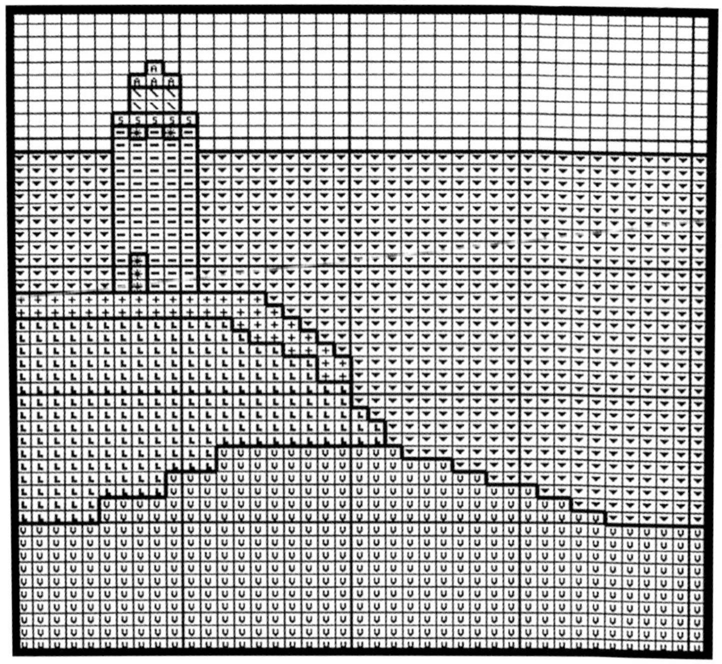

READ PURL ROWS FROM THIS SIDE

READ KNIT ROWS FROM THIS SIDE

GRAPH 9

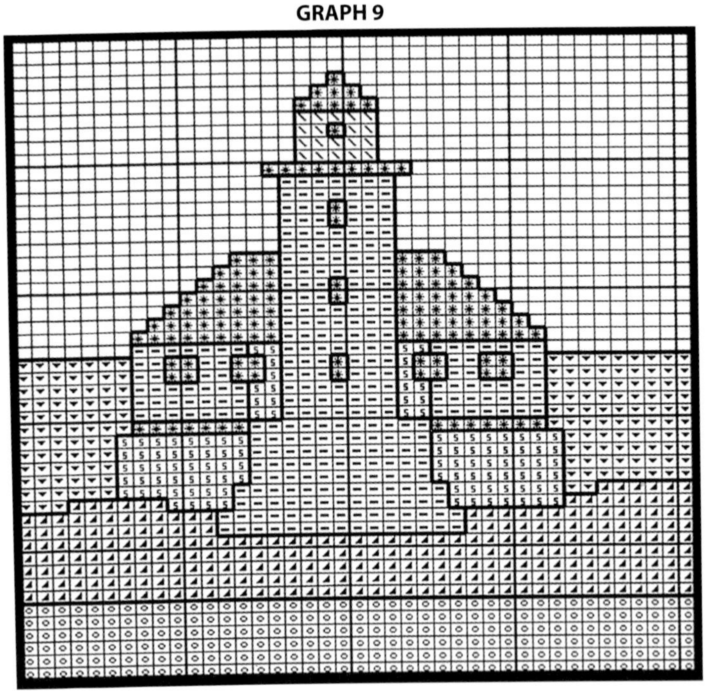

READ PURL ROWS FROM THIS SIDE

READ KNIT ROWS FROM THIS SIDE

GRAPH 10

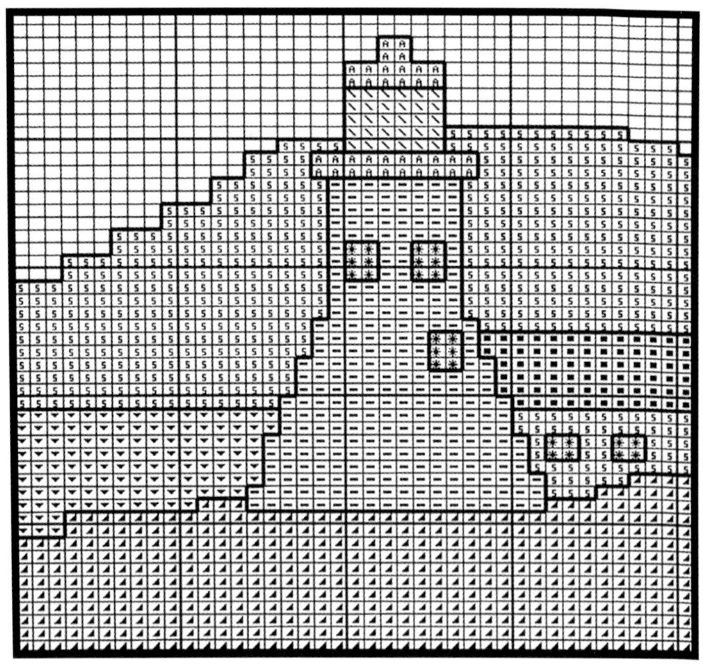

READ PURL ROWS FROM THIS SIDE

READ KNIT ROWS FROM THIS SIDE

GRAPH A

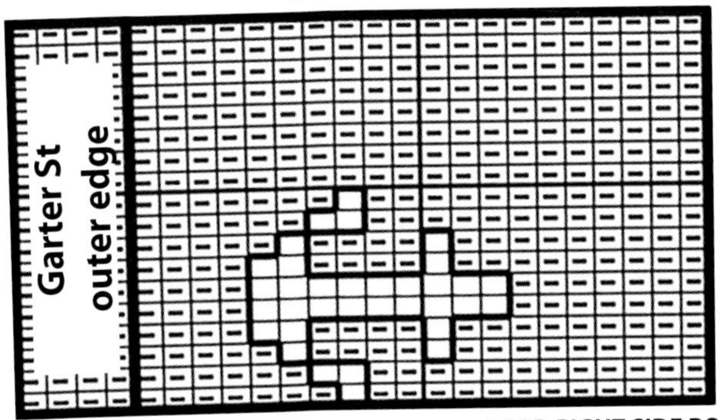

GRAPH B

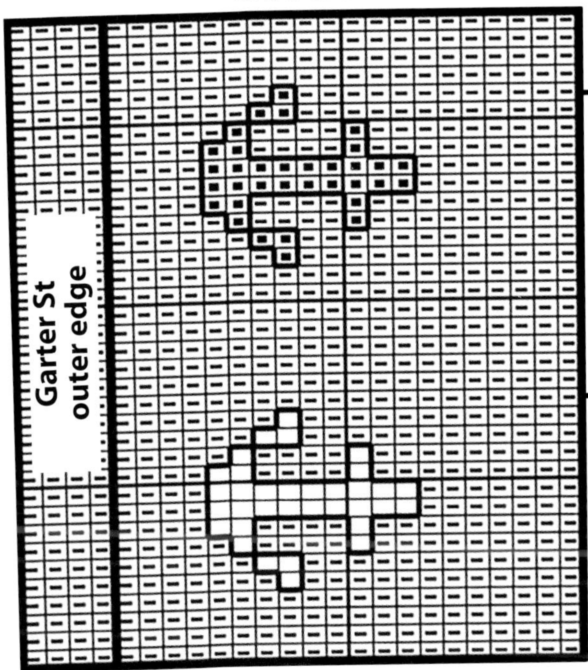

GRAPH C

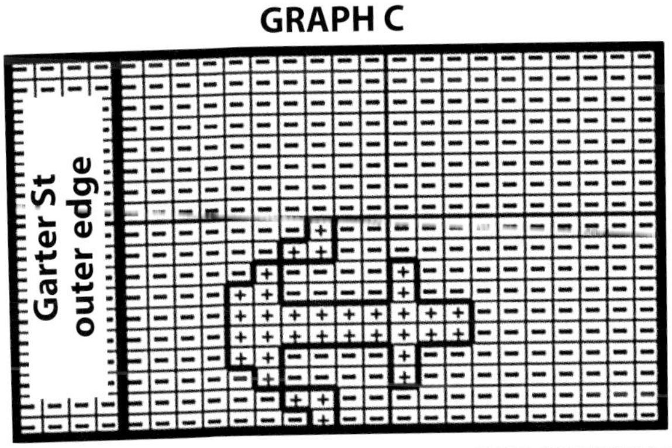

COLOR KEY

MC	—	White
Color 1		Lt Blue
Color 2	▼	Dk Blue
Color 3	■	Dk Brown
Color 4	+	Lt Green
Color 5	L	Dk Green
Color 6	o	Sand
Color 7	U	Lt Brown
Color 8	\	Yellow
Color 9	A	Red
Color 10	S	Lt Grey
Color 11	◢	Med Grey
Color 12	*	Black

NOTE: Every square on the graph represents a stitch. Changes in color are shown by different symbols. Follow graph from right to left for knit rows and left to right for purl rows.

Placement Diagram

Color 10	**Graph 6**	**Color 2**	**Graph 1**	**Color 9**
Graph 3	**Color 4**	**Graph 7**	**Color 7**	**Graph 4**
Color 8	**Graph 9**	**Color 5**	**Graph 5**	**Color 11**
Graph 10	**Color 1**	**Graph 2**	**Color 6**	**Graph 8**

Fall Foliage Afghan

INTERMEDIATE

SHOPPING LIST

Yarn (Worsted Weight) MEDIUM 4

Mary Maxim Best Value

[6 ounces, 342 yards

(170 grams, 312 meters) per skein]:

☐ Merlot 11 skeins

Knitting Needles

36" (90 cm) Circular Needle

☐ Size 8 (5.00 mm)

SIZE INFORMATION

Finished: 46" x 62" [117 x 157.5 cm]

GAUGE INFORMATION

One repeat (22 sts) = 3 1/2" measured over pattern using **suggested** needle or any size needle which will give the correct stitch gauge or tension.

TO SAVE TIME, TAKE TIME TO CHECK GAUGE

STITCH GUIDE

C2B: Slip next st onto cable needle and hold at back of work, k1, then k1 from cable needle.

M3: (K1, p1, k1) all into next st - makes 3 sts from one st.

KB1: Knit into back of next st.

SKP: Slip 1, knit 1, pass slipped stitch over knit stitch.

SK2P: Slip 1, k2tog, pass slipped stitch over.

INSTRUCTIONS

To Make: Cast on 199 sts and knit 17 rows .

Next Row: (inc row) K 10, PM, k5, *inc one st in next st, k1; rep from * to 16 sts, k6, PM, k 10 - 283 sts.

Now keeping first 10 sts and last 10 sts in Garter st as set - every row k, work Leaf Pattern over center 263 sts only as follows:

Row 1: (right side) P2, C2B, p2, k2, SKP, yo, k1, yo, k2tog, k2, p2, C2B, p2, *KB1, p2, C2B, p2, k2, SKP, yo, k1, yo, k2tog, k2, p2, C2B, p2; rep from * to last marker.

Row 2: K2, p2, k2, p9, k2, p2, k2, *p1, k2, p2, k2, p9, k2, p2, k2; rep from * to last marker.

Row 3: P2, C2B, p2, SKP, k5, k2tog, p2, C2B, p2, *M3, p2, C2B, p2, SKP, k5, k2tog, p2, C2B, p2; rep from * to last marker - 281 sts.

Row 4: K2, p2, k2, p7, k2, p2, k2, *p3, k2, p2, k2, p7, k2, p2, k2; rep from * to last marker.

Row 5: P2, C2B, p2, SKP, k3, k2tog, p2, C2B, p2, *k1, [yo, k1] twice, p2, C2B, p2, SKP, k3, k2tog, p2, C2B, p2; rep from * to last marker - 279 sts.

Row 6: K2, p2, k2, *p5, k2, p2, k2; rep from * to last marker.

Row 7: P2, C2B, p2, SKP, k1, k2tog, p2, C2B, p2, *k2, yo, k1, yo, k2, p2, C2B, p2, SKP, k1, k2tog, p2, C2B, p2; rep from * to last marker - 277 sts.

Row 8: K2, p2, k2, p3, k2, p2, k2, *p7, k2, p2, k2, p3, k2, p2, k2; rep from * to last marker.

Row 9: P2, C2B, p2, SK2P, p2, C2B, p2, *k3, yo, k1, yo, k3, p2, C2B, p2, SK2P, p2, C2B, p2; rep from * to last marker - 275 sts.

Row 10: K2, p2, k2, p1, k2, p2, k2, *p9, k2, p2, k2, p1, k2, p2, k2; rep from * to last marker.

Row 11: P2, C2B, p2, KB1, p2, C2B, p2, *k2, SKP, yo, k1, yo, k2tog, k2, p2, C2B, p2, KB1, p2, C2B, p2; rep from * to last marker.

Row 12: Repeat Row 10.

Row 13: P2, C2B, p2, M3, p2, C2B, p2, *SKP, k5, k2tog, p2, C2B, p2, M3, p2, C2B, p2; rep from * to last marker - 277 sts.

Row 14: Repeat Row 8.

Row 15: P2, C2B, p2, k1, [yo, k1] twice, p2, C2B, p2, *SKP, k3, k2tog, p2, C2B, p2, k1, [yo, k1] twice, p2, C2B, p2; rep from * to last marker - 279 sts.

Row 16: Repeat Row 6.

Row 17: P2, C2B, p2, k2, yo, k1, yo, k2, p2, C2B, p2, *SKP, k1, k2tog, p2, C2B, p2, k2, yo, k1, yo, k2, p2, C2B, p2; rep from * to last marker - 281 sts.

Row 18: Repeat Row 4.

Row 19: P2, C2B, p2, k3, yo, k1, yo, k3, p2, C2B, p2, *SK2P, p2, C2B, p2, k3, yo, k1, yo, k3, p2, C2B, p2; rep from * to last marker - 283 sts.

Row 20: Repeat Row 2.

Repeat these 20 rows of Leaf Pattern until afghan measures about 60" [152.5 cm] from cast on edge, ending after a Row 20 and removing all markers on last row.

Next Row: (dec row) K 15, *k2tog, k1; rep from * to last 16 sts, k 16 - 199 sts.

Knit 17 rows. Cast off knitwise.

Weave in all ends.

Design by Billie Birchfield.

General Instructions

ABBREVIATIONS

"	inches
approx.	approximately
beg	begin or beginning
CC	Contrast Color
cm	centimeters
dec	decrease or decreasing
inc	increase or increasing
k	knit
p	purl
psso	pass slipped stitch over
M	marker
MC	Main Color
mm	milimeters
rem	remain or remaining
rep	repeat
rnd	round
sl	slip
st	stitch
sts	stitches
St st	Stocking stitch
tbl	through back loop
tog	together
yds	yards
yo	yarn over

SYMBOLS & TERMS

*** or #** work instructions following or between * or # as many more times as indicated in addition to the first time.

() or [ ] work enclosed instructions as many times as specified by the number immediately following **or** work all enclosed instructions in the stitch or space indicated **or** contains explanatory remarks

— the number(s) given after a hyphen at the end of a row or round denote(s) the number of stitches or spaces you should have on that row or round.

Yarn Weight Symbol & Names	LACE 0	SUPER FINE 1	FINE 2	LIGHT 3	MEDIUM 4	BULKY 5	SUPER BULKY 6
Type of Yarns in Category	Fingering, size 10 crochet thread	Sock, Fingering, Baby	Sport, Baby	DK, Light Worsted	Worsted, Afghan, Aran	Chunky, Craft, Rug	Bulky, Roving
Knit Gauge Range* in Stockinette St to 4" (10 cm)	33-40** sts	27-32 sts	23-26 sts	21-24 sts	16-20 sts	12-15 sts	6-11 sts
Advised Needle Size Range	000-1	1 to 3	3 to 5	5 to 7	7 to 9	9 to 11	11 and larger

*GUIDELINES ONLY: The chart above reflects the most commonly used gauges and needle sizes for specific yarn categories.

KNIT TERMINOLOGY		
UNITED STATES		INTERNATIONAL
gauge	=	tension
bind off	=	cast off

BEGINNER	Projects for first-time knitters using basic knit and purl stitches. Minimal shaping.
EASY	Projects using basic stitches, repetitive stitch patterns, simple color changes, and simple shaping and finishing.
INTERMEDIATE	Projects with a variety of stitches, such as basic cables and lace, simple intarsia, double-pointed needles and knitting in the round needle techniques, mid-level shaping and finishing.
EXPERIENCED	Projects using advanced techniques and stitches, such as short rows, fair isle, more intricate intarsia, cables, lace patterns and numerous color changes.

KNITTING NEEDLES

U.S.	50	35	19	17	15	13	11	----	----	10.5	10	9	8	7	6	5	4	3	----	2	1	0	----
U.K.	---	----	----	----	000	00	0	1	2	3	4	5	6	7	8	9	----	10	11	12	13	14	15
Metric mm	25	19	15	12.75	10	9	8	7.5	7	6.5	6	5.5	5	4.5	4	3.75	3.5	3.25	3	2.75	2.25	2	1.75

Casting On

1A

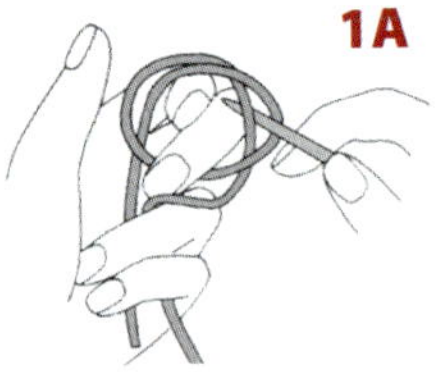

1B

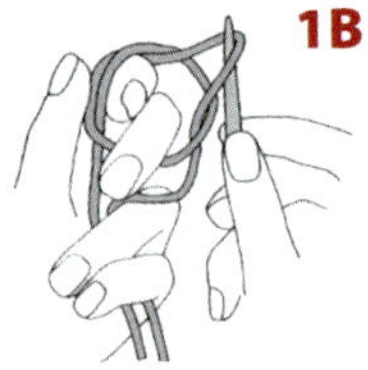

3A

3B

1A. Make a slip knot: Loop the yarn as shown and slip needle under the lower strand of the loop.

1B. Pull up a loop of yarn.

2. Pull the yarn end attached to the ball of yarn to tighten the slip knot leaving the other end approx. 4" [10 cm] long. Transfer needle to left hand.

3A. Insert the right-hand needle through slip knot and wind yarn over right-hand needle.

3B. Pull loop through slip knot.

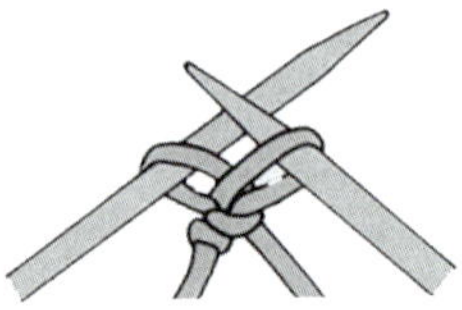

4. Place new loop on left-handle needle. (You now have 2 stitches (sts) on your left-hand needle.)

5. Insert right-hand needle between last 2 stitches (sts) on left-hand needle and wind yarn over right-hand needle.

6. Pull loop through. Place this new loop on left-hand needle beside last stitch (st). (You now have 1 more stitch on left-hand needle.) Repeat (rep) steps 5 and 6 until required number of stitches (sts) have been cast on left-hand needle.

The Knit Stitch

1. Hold the needle with cast on stitches (sts) in your left hand, and the loose yarn attached to the ball at the back of work. Insert right-hand needle from left to right through the front of the first stitch (st) on the left-hand needle.

2. Wind the yarn from left to right over the point of the right-hand needle.

3. Draw the yarn through this original stitch (st) which forms a new stitch (st) on right-hand needle.

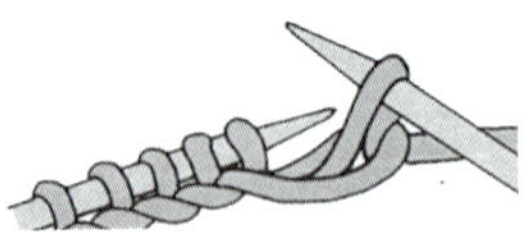

4. Slip the original stitch (st) off the left-hand needle, keeping the new stitch (st) on the right-hand needle.

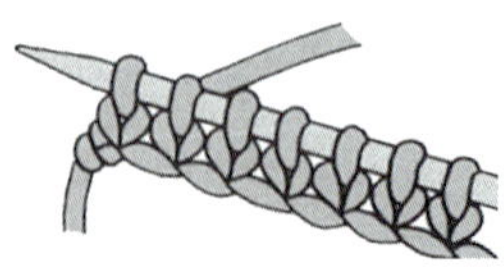

5. To knit a row, repeat steps 1 to 4 until all stitches (sts) have been transferred from left-hand needle to right-hand needle. Turn the work by transferring the needle with stitches (sts) into your left hand to knit the next row.

The Purl Stitch

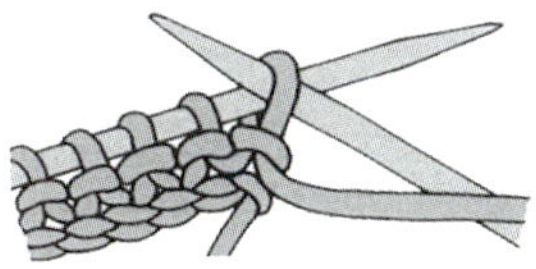

1. With yarn at front of work, insert right-hand needle from right to left through front of first stitch (st) on left-hand needle.

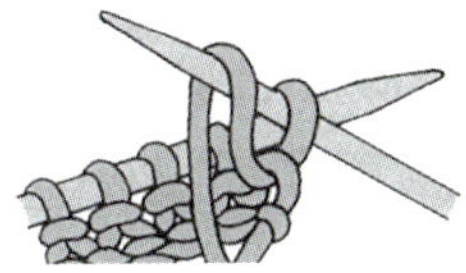

2. Wind yarn around right-hand needle. Pull yarn through stitch (st).

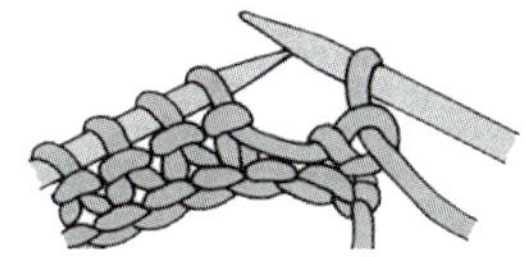

3. Slip original stitch (st) off needle. Repeat (rep) these steps until all stitches (sts) on left-hand needle have been transferred onto right-hand needle to complete one row of purling.

Increasing and Decreasing

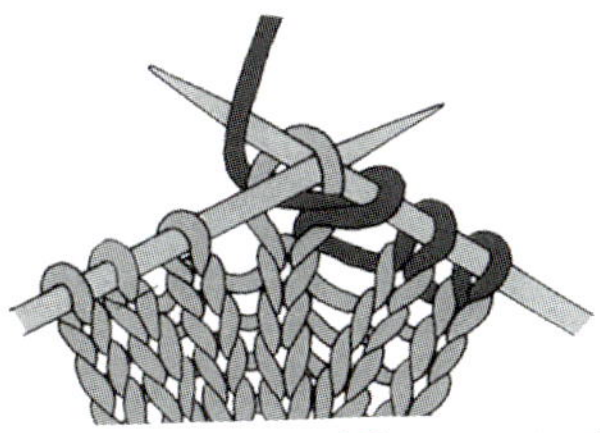

Increase 1 stitch (st) in next stitch (st): Work into front and back of stitch (st) as follows: Knit stitch (st), then before slipping it off needle, twist right-hand needle behind left-hand needle and knit again into back of loop. Slip original stitch (st) off needle. There are now 2 stitches (sts) on right-hand needle made from original stitch.

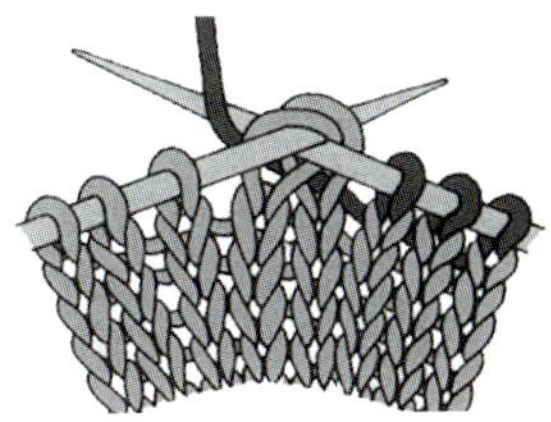

K2tog Decrease: Knit 2 stitches (sts) together (tog) through the front of both loops.

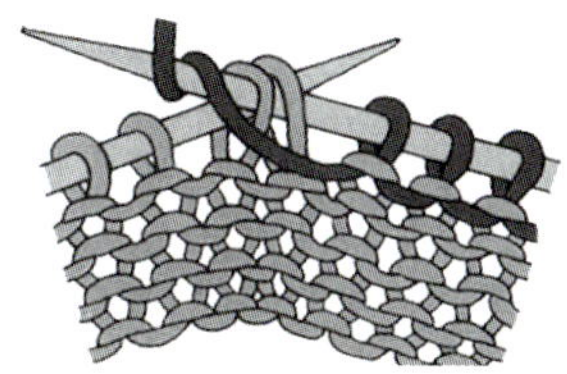

P2tog Decrease: Purl 2 stitches (sts) together (tog) through the front of both loops.

Casting Off

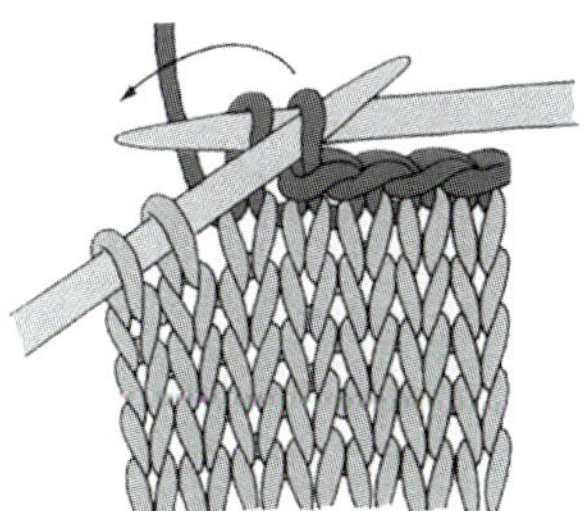

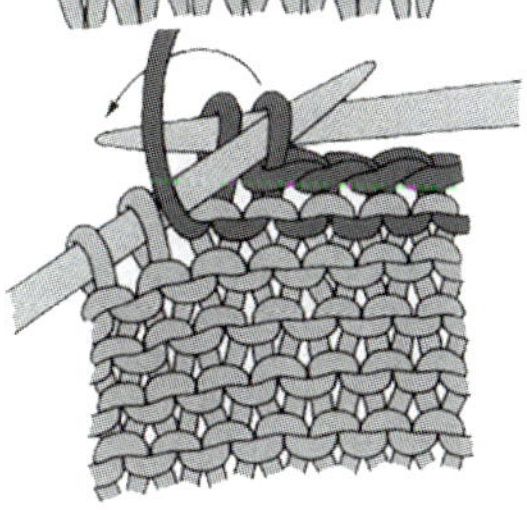

Cast off using knit stitch (knitwise): Knit the first 2 stitches (sts). *Using left-hand needle, lift first stitch (st) over second stitch (st) and drop it off between points of the 2 needles. Knit the next stitch (st); repeat (rep) from * until all stitches (sts) from left-hand needle have been worked and only 1 stitch (st) remains on the right-hand needle. Cut yarn (leaving enough to sew in end) and thread cut end through stitch (st) on needle. Draw yarn up firmly to fasten off last stitch (st).

Cast off using purl stitch (purlwise): Purl first 2 stitches (sts). *Using left-hand needle, lift first stitch (st) over second stitch (st) and drop it off needle. Purl next stitch (st) as described for casting off knitwise.

Yarn Information

Projects in this book were made with medium weight yarns. Any brand of yarn may be used. It is best to refer to yardage/meters when determining how many balls or skeins to purchase. Remember, to arrive at the finished size, it is the GAUGE/TENSION that is important, not the brand of yarn. For your convenience, listed below are the specific yarn ranges used to create our photographed models.

Aran Textures and Cables Afghan and Pillow
Mary Maxim® Starlette®

Log Cabin Throw
Mary Maxim® Starlette®

Zig Zag Throw
Mary Maxim® Best Value®

Cable Panels Throw
Mary Maxim® Starlette® Tweed

Lighthouses Afghan
Red Heart® Super Saver®

Fall Foliage Afghan
Mary Maxim® Best Value®

Every effort has been made to have the directions contained in this pattern accurate and complete; however, we cannot be responsible for misinterpretation, variance or errors in workmanship of the individual.